Author:

Fiona Macdonald studied history at Cambridge University, England, and at the University of East Anglia. She has taught in schools, adult education and universities, and is the author of numerous books for children on historical topics.

Artist:

David Antram was born in Brighton, England, in 1958. He studied at Eastbourne College of Art and then worked in advertising for 15 years before becoming a full-time artist. He has illustrated many children's non-fiction books.

Series creator:

David Salariya was born in Dundee, Scotland. He has illustrated a wide range of books and has created and designed many new series for publishers in the UK and overseas. David established The Salariya Book Company in 1989. He lives in Brighton with his wife, illustrator Shirley Willis, and their son Jonathan.

Editor: Victoria England

Editorial Assistant: Mark Williams

Visit
www.salariya.com
for our online catalogue and **free** interactive web books.

Published in Great Britain in MMXIV by Book House, an imprint of
The Salariya Book Company Ltd
25 Marlborough Place, Brighton BN1 1UB
www.salariya.com
www.book-house.co.uk

HB ISBN-13: 978-1-908973-79-5
PB ISBN-13: 978-1-908973-80-1

SALARIYA

A CIP catalogue record for this book is available from the British Library.

Printed and bound in China.

Visit our website at **www.book-house.co.uk** or go to **www.salariya.com** for **free** electronic versions of:
You Wouldn't Want to be an Egyptian Mummy!
You Wouldn't Want to be a Roman Gladiator!
You Wouldn't Want to be a Polar Explorer!
You Wouldn't Want to sail on a 19th-Century Whaling Ship!

PAPER FROM
SUSTAINABLE
FORESTS

Avoid being a worker on the Taj Mahal!

Written by
Fiona Macdonald

Illustrated by
David Antram

Created and designed by
David Salariya

The Danger Zone™

BOOK HOUSE
a SALARIYA *imprint*

Contents

Introduction

One in twenty thousand – that's you! You're a hard-working, poorly paid labourer, living in north India around 1632. You have a wife and children to support, and elderly parents, too. Right now, there are few jobs in your village. You try as hard as you can, but you often don't earn enough to keep body and soul together.

By chance, one day, you meet a convoy of merchants heading for the city of Agra. They tell you that Emperor Shah Jahan is planning a huge new monument there – and is looking for twenty thousand workers to build it! This grand construction will be called the Taj Mahal.* It's to be a place of prayer, a loving memorial and a beautiful tomb. Agra is a long, long way from your village, but you decide to risk the journey…

See you in a few years!

The name means 'Crown of Palaces'.

The Favourite of the Palace

I t's a wrench leaving your family. Some workers take wives and children with them, but you decide to go alone. You travel on foot, hitching lifts on bullock-carts if you can. It's summer and the burning sun blazes down. But as you trek along dry and dusty roads towards Agra, you hear a very romantic story. The Taj Mahal will be the resting place of wise, clever, beautiful Mumtaz Mahal, third wife of Emperor Shah Jahan. Unlike most royal couples, they were truly, madly, deeply in love. But Mumtaz Mahal died last year, and the Emperor is grief-stricken.

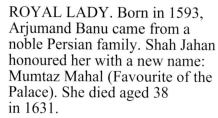

ROYAL LADY. Born in 1593, Arjumand Banu came from a noble Persian family. Shah Jahan honoured her with a new name: Mumtaz Mahal (Favourite of the Palace). She died aged 38 in 1631.

Not just a pretty face

MUMTAZ MAHAL was more than just beautiful…

She offered good advice…

…*and* toured the Mughal Empire to support her husband…

…*and* kept a watchful eye on palace quarrels and rival politicians…

…*and* gave generously to poor people *and* encouraged religion, learning and the arts.

LOVING LORD. Born in 1592, Shah Jahan was the son of Mughal emperor Jahangir. Although his marriage was arranged, he fell in love with Mumtaz Mahal soon after meeting her, and stayed in love throughout their life together.

Handy hint

Don't be too beautiful. You'll be loved too much. Mumtaz Mahal died giving birth to her 14th child.

What a woman!

Tell me your troubles. I can help!

The Ruler of the World

As you get close to Agra, you also learn more about sorrowful Shah Jahan. At first glance, he seems to have everything. He's healthy, handsome, rich, intelligent, brave, popular, a fine soldier, a strong ruler, and a lover of architecture, art and gardens. He collects books, paintings and exquisite jewels. His parents named him Prince Khurram; his conquests have earned him the proud title Shah Jahan (Ruler of the World). But death defeats even princes, and now he has lost his greatest treasure, his beloved Mumtaz Mahal. The Taj Mahal will be a tribute to her, a 'poem in stone'.

The first Mughal emperors

1526–1530 Babur: Conquers north India, founds empire.
1530–1540 Humayun: Young and weak – but loves poetry.
1540–1555 Riots and rebellions.
1555–1556 Humayun wins back power.
1556–1605 Akbar the Great: World class! Wins land, reforms government, loves the arts, likes religious toleration.
1605–1628 Jahangir: Rebels against his father, promotes Urdu language, develops trade with Europe.
1628–1666 Shah Jahan
1666–1707 Aurangzeb: Great warrior; strictly devoted to Islam.
After 1707 Mughal power fades away. But the Mughal Empire struggles on until 1857.

Handy hint

Put your family first. It's said that Mumtaz Mahal asked Shah Jahan not to have babies with his other wives, so that her children would inherit his empire.

WHO ARE THE MUGHALS? Central Asian warlords, descended from fearsome Mongol emperor Genghis Khan (died 1227). Along with ruthless battle techniques, they bring Persian and Mongol traditions to India, creating a new and brilliant culture that flourishes for 200 years.

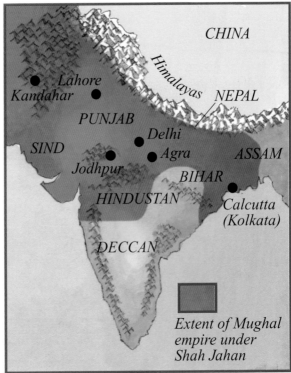

Extent of Mughal empire under Shah Jahan

THE MUGHAL EMPIRE stretches for over 2.5 million square km, from Persia (Iran) in the West to Nepal in the East. Mughal emperors fight local kings and princes to conquer land and win treasure, but find their vast empire very difficult to defend.

Thinking big

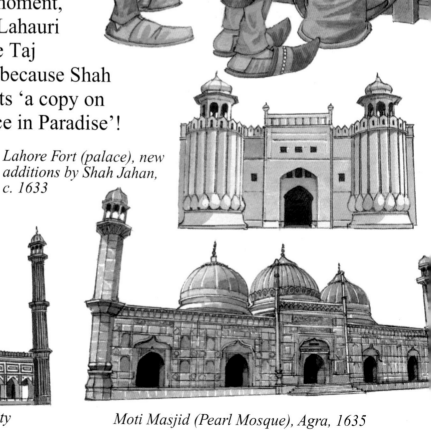

You don't know this, but you're living in the 'Golden Age of Mughal Architecture'. Shah Jahan loves to give orders for new buildings; they win him honour and fame, and increase the glory of his empire. He's got the knowledge and good taste to employ the best workers – and the money to pay them. With luck, soon you'll become a (very junior) member of his world-class team. At the moment, chief architect Ustad Ahmad Lahauri is busy with final plans for the Taj Mahal. It's an awesome task, because Shah Jahan is thinking big. He wants 'a copy on earth of the soul's resting place in Paradise'!

SHAH JAHAN'S Mughal monuments combine international features such as Persian *iwans* (grand entrance halls), Turkish domes, Muslim minarets and delicate Hindu carvings.

Lahore Fort (palace), new additions by Shah Jahan, c. 1633

Jama Masjid (mosque for community prayers), Delhi, 1650–1656

Moti Masjid (Pearl Mosque), Agra, 1635

THE TAJ MAHAL will be set in a carefully designed landscape with gardens, terraces, grand gateways and outer pavilions. The River Yamuna runs close by. The Taj Mahal will appear as a delicate reflection in its waters.

Handy hint

Break with tradition! Previous Mughal rulers built wonderful tombs, but the Taj Mahal is the first great tomb in India to be built for a woman.

Moonlight Gardens

River Yamuna

Taj Mahal

Paradise Gardens

Red Fort (Shah Jahan's new palace), Delhi, 1638–1648

Diwan-i-Khas (private reception hall), Delhi, 1638–1648

11

Join the queue

At last you reach Agra, Shah Jahan's capital city. It's astonishingly crowded – you've never seen so many people! They come from all over the Mughal Empire, and speak many different languages. Some are Muslims, like Shah Jahan and Mumtaz Mahal; some are Hindus or Christians. Most are simple labourers, but you also see proud, well-trained craftsmen with expert skills.

You weave your way through the crowds, and find shabby lodgings in a shared room in the workers' district, Mumtazabad. Then you stand in line, for days and days, waiting your turn to join the building team.

Expert craftsmen

SHAH JAHAN has recruited expert craftworkers from Central Asia, the Indian subcontinent, Iran, Turkey, Syria – and Europe! All have spent many years studying, training and perfecting their skills.

Mason   *Stone cutter*   *Carver*   *Inlayer of precious stones*   *Painter*

It takes all sorts...

Handy hint

Be open-minded! Show respect! You'll meet many people whose way of life is different from your own. But remember, you're all part of the same team.

Calligrapher   Gold worker   Garden designer

Begin at the bottom

A ha! At last! You've been given work to do. You've joined the team building foundations for the Taj Mahal. These have to be extra strong, because the River Yamuna is nearby. Every year, after the summer monsoon, its waters burst their banks. The floods must not sweep the new tomb away! You dig a huge hole and lay wooden drainpipes to carry floodwater back to the river. You add ventilation shafts to let trapped air escape, and then fill the hole with gravel. It's essential work – but exhausting. Admiring visitors say that workers' hands are strong as steel!

WHO'S PAYING? Building the Taj Mahal will cost 32 million rupees* – and is emptying Shah Jahan's treasury. Since the time of Akbar, Mughal emperors have issued beautiful gold coins to encourage trade, and collected taxes to pay for their government and army. But now Shah Jahan is demanding more!

Today this would be worth about £680 million (US$ 1 billion).

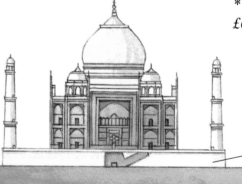

Lower plinth

Upper platform

Foundations

A SOLID START. Once the drainpipes are laid and the huge hole is back-filled, you add a layer of crushed stone to create a smooth, firm surface. On top, you build a huge stone plinth (platform), 190 m long, 71 m wide and 8 m high. This will soon be topped by a smaller platform for the Taj Mahal to stand on.

Will you build in red, for royalty...?

For the mighty Mughal dynasty, red is the colour of royalty. Mughal emperors hold court in rich red tents on battlefields, and when they go hunting. The lower plinth that you've just helped build is made of deep red sandstone. Now you're busy building a smaller platform on top, out of red mud bricks dried in the hot sun then baked in huge bonfires. The strong walls and domed roof of the Taj Mahal will be made of brickwork, too. And so is the builders' scaffolding. Why? There's not enough suitable material nearby to make ordinary scaffolding of bamboo or wood.

Ten million and one, ten million and two...

Handy hint

The mortar must be mixed with edible ingredients, such as molasses or whey. They make the mortar stickier and the brick structure stronger.

Brick making

MASS PRODUCTION. Bricks used to build the Taj Mahal are made of sticky natural clay squeezed into moulds so that they will all be a standard size: around 12 cm wide, 3 cm deep and 18 cm long.

Sandstone

DRESS YOUR BEST! Already, bullock-drivers are bringing blocks of red sandstone from local quarries. These will be used to dress (cover) the brick platform, and build protective walls.

Using wedges to split the stone

...or in white, to shine like the moon?

All night, the monsoon rains have drummed on the roof of your room. Unable to sleep, you get up and reach the building site long before your team leader. You find the experts already hard at work, constructing tall, tapering minarets together with Persian-style iwans (entrance halls) and *pishtaqs* (tall arched gateways). To Muslims, a single-pointed arch is a sign of the One True God. These wonders are built of brick but clad in translucent white marble. At dawn and dusk, its gleaming surface shines like the moon. It's a symbol of death – and of paradise.

AT THE QUARRY, workers cut marble into blocks weighing 6 tonnes. Then elephants haul the blocks to the building site.

IN THE PATTERN known as 'Mughal bond', thin strips of white marble are laid between blocks of red sandstone.

THE MAUSOLEUM at the Taj Mahal will hold Mumtaz Mahal's public tomb. Underneath, there will be a private chamber, where her body will be buried. Outside the mausoleum, there will be four tall minarets (towers for calling Muslims to prayer).

Iwan
Pishtaq   *Minaret*

Handy hint

Build the minarets just outside the main platform. If they collapse (as minarets sometimes do) they'll fall outwards and not damage the mausoleum.

Yikes!

Linking Earth with Heaven

ongratulations! You've been promoted. Now you've joined the team building the roof of the Taj Mahal. Let's hope you have a good head for heights! Shah Jahan's clever architects have designed a beautiful *amrud* (guava-shaped) dome to go above the mausoleum.

Four smaller domed structures, called *chattris*, surround it; their arched windows let light into the mausoleum below. To Muslims, the dome shape links this world with Paradise; it is also a reminder of the pearl-roofed throne where God sits to judge dead souls. The dome is topped by a beautiful finial (spire), made of pure gold, pointing upwards towards the heavens.

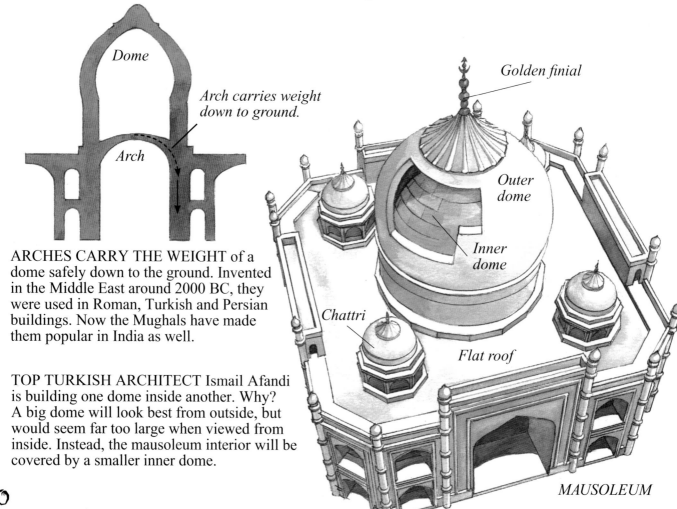

Dome

Arch carries weight down to ground.

Arch

Golden finial

Outer dome

Inner dome

Chattri

Flat roof

ARCHES CARRY THE WEIGHT of a dome safely down to the ground. Invented in the Middle East around 2000 BC, they were used in Roman, Turkish and Persian buildings. Now the Mughals have made them popular in India as well.

TOP TURKISH ARCHITECT Ismail Afandi is building one dome inside another. Why? A big dome will look best from outside, but would seem far too large when viewed from inside. Instead, the mausoleum interior will be covered by a smaller inner dome.

MAUSOLEUM

Handy hint

Learn from local people! The lotus-flower bud on the finial is borrowed from local Hindu artistic traditions. It is a sign of beauty and purity.

THE GOLDEN FINIAL on the Taj Mahal dome soars 73 metres above the ground. It is topped by a crescent moon (the symbol of Islam) and a lotus-flower bud.

I'm heading for the heights of my profession!

Are you calm enough to be a carver?

You'll need a steady hand! Now the dome is finished, you've been sent to help craftsmen decorating the mausoleum. You'll run errands for them, and carry heavy loads.

You gaze in awe as the carvers fit pieces of coloured stone together to make geometric patterns, or incise (cut) dazzling designs. With amazing skill, the lapidaries set lifelike flowers into white marble, using gems from many lands: purple amethysts, yellow amber, red coral, green jade, deep blue lapis lazuli and more. You hear that the goldsmiths have been making a jewel-encrusted screen to surround Mumtaz Mahal's public tomb. See – here it comes!

Decorative techniques

SACRED MESSAGES. Inside and out, the walls of the Taj Mahal are covered with decorations. Most are full of religious meanings – but they are also exquisitely beautiful.

LAPIDARIES come from Bukhara in Central Asia. They sketch designs on marble using henna dye, then chisel them out and fill the spaces with precisely cut coloured stones.

Phew! Gold's almost twice as heavy as lead, you know!

STONECUTTERS draw leaves and flowers on polished marble, then trim away the background.

Handy hint

Be wise and use flower patterns. They'll remind visitors of the short-lived pleasures of this life, and the eternal glories of Paradise.

EVEN THE FLOORS are works of art. Marble tiles are arranged in stunning shapes.

MUSLIM TRADITION bans pictures of living people and animals, because only God can create life.

IN HER LIFETIME, Mumtaz Mahal was hidden from view behind delicate carved stone screens. This *jali* stonework also decorates the Taj Mahal.

INSIDE THE MAUSOLEUM, Mumtaz Mahal's public tomb (right and below) takes pride of place. But her body rests in a private chamber underneath. Her casket is simple; she lies facing the holy city of Mecca.

Words of wonder

O n your way home after work, you pass through the bazaar. You see craftsmen with panels of graceful Arabic inscriptions. Their creator, Persian calligrapher Abd al-Haqq, is so good that Shah Jahan calls him Amanat Khan (Trusted Lord). For the inscriptions, Amanat Khan has chosen texts from the Muslim holy book, the Qur'an. Their theme is God's judgement on sinful souls. On Mumtaz Mahal's public tomb, he will write the Ninety-Nine Names of God.

How the calligraphy is done

FIVE YEARS OF WRITING (1632–c.1637)

FOR MUSLIMS, copying holy texts is a religious action, like meditating or saying prayers.

CHOOSE TEXTS carefully as your work will be seen by pilgrims and visitors for hundreds of years.

OUTLINE THE letters on smooth white marble using a reed pen and paint made from henna.

CUT OUT THE shape of each letter. You are also creating an elegant, flowing pattern.

WITH SKILL and dedication, you cut the same letter shapes from black marble.

FINALLY, gently fit the black letters into the spaces you have cut in the white marble.

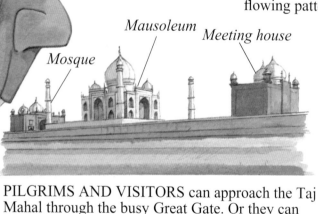

Mosque · Mausoleum · Meeting house

PILGRIMS AND VISITORS can approach the Taj Mahal through the busy Great Gate. Or they can stop and rest at the Taj Mahal meeting house, and say their prayers at the Taj Mahal mosque.

Handy hint

Make it legible!
Amanat Khan
changes the size
of his writing
depending on its
distance from the ground.
That way, it looks regular
wherever it is viewed from.

Planting a Paradise garden

Phew! What a scorcher! Surrounded by hot, dusty stones, you'd love to change places with gardeners working beside the cool River Yamuna. Time has passed; it's now 1640 and the Taj Mahal buildings are nearing completion. So Shah Jahan has ordered beautiful gardens all around them; for Muslims, these will be reminders of Paradise. Already, gardeners have dug flowerbeds, and builders have constructed a long canal with pools and fountains. Soon there will be exotic birds, ornamental fish, tall cypress trees (symbols of love), and fruit trees (signs of life).

COME THIS WAY. The main entrance to the Taj Mahal faces the long Paradise Gardens. Behind, on the far river bank, the Moonlight Gardens offer romantic reflections of its domes and towers by night.

The end – and a beginning

It's 1648 – and the Taj Mahal is finished. Will you go home? Or will you join the labourers on Shah Jahan's next building project? He's planning a whole new city 200 km south of Agra: Shajahanabad (now Delhi). He's already left Agra, but has given orders for special prayers every year on the day Mumtaz Mahal died. He has had her body moved from its temporary grave to the Taj Mahal mausoleum. And he plans to be buried there, beside her.

UNHAPPY ENDING. Shah Jahan's reign ends in tragedy. His sons fight. The strongest, Aurangzeb, takes over the Mughal Empire in 1658 and puts Shah Jahan in prison. In 1666, Shah Jahan dies, gazing from his deathbed at the 'teardrop on the cheek of eternity' (as a famous Indian poet called the Taj Mahal much later).

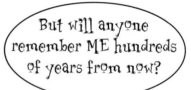

But will anyone remember ME hundreds of years from now?

FUTURE FEARS. Over three million tourists visit the Taj Mahal each year. But polluting fumes from modern India's factories have damaged its stonework, and recent climate change is drying out the ground and may now threaten its foundations.

His *Hers*

TOGETHER FOREVER.
Shah Jahan has paid for his
own magnificent public tomb
to stand in the Taj Mahal
mausoleum. But his body will
be laid to rest beside Mumtaz
Mahal, in their peaceful,
private burial chamber.

Handy hint

It would cost a
fortune to demolish
the brick scaffolding,
so free bricks are
offered to
anyone who
can carry
them.

Glossary

Amrud dome A dome in the shape of a guava fruit, which looks like an onion or a teardrop.

Calligrapher A craft worker who creates beautiful writing.

Ceramic Made of clay.

Chattri A dome standing on pillars (usually four), often built on the roof of a mosque or temple. In India, larger chattris were built as memorials.

Convoy A group of people or vehicles travelling together.

Finial A decoration, often pointed, fixed to the top of a post, arch or building.

Henna A plant that grows in India and nearby lands. Its powdered leaves produce a rusty-red dye.

Hindu A person who follows the ancient faith and customs of the Indian subcontinent. Hindus worship many gods. They honour *dharma* (the natural law of the universe), believe in *karma* (that your good or bad actions will reward or punish you), and hope to find *mokshi* or *nirvana* (spiritual peace and freedom).

Inscription Writing cut or carved into stone, wood or other long-lasting material.

Iwan A building (such as an entrance hall or archway) that has walls on three sides, but one side open. Usually covered by an arched or domed roof.

Jali An Indian craft technique that creates delicate lacy patterns in stone.

Lapidary A craft worker who cuts and polishes jewels and decorative stones.

Lotus A kind of water-lily.

Mausoleum A house for the dead.

Meditating Thinking very deeply about spiritual matters.

Minaret A tall tower, part of a mosque, from which Muslims are called to say prayers.

Mongols A nomadic people who lived in Central Asia. Under leaders such as Genghis Khan, they ruled a vast empire in the 13th and 14th centuries AD.

Monsoon A period of very heavy rainfall that happens at around the same time each year. At Agra, the monsoon season is from July to September.

Mortar A mixture of crushed, burned limestone, water and sand. It sets hard and is used to stick bricks or stones together.

Mosque A building where Muslims meet to pray and hear readings from the Qur'an. The name means 'a place of bowing down'.

Mughal Descended from Mongols (the two words mean the same). Prince Babur founded the Mughal Empire in India in 1526.

Muslim A person who worships Allah (the One True God) and honours Muhammad as God's Prophet (religious guide). Muslims also honour and respect a holy book, the Qur'an.

Pavilions Smaller buildings, often designed for rest or pleasure, standing close to a more important structure.

Persian From Persia (today known as Iran), a land with a long history and a rich civilisation, on the borders of the Mughal empire.

Pishtaq A gateway added to the front of a building, usually in the shape of a high, decorated arch. Originally a Persian or Iraqi architectural style.

Plinth A platform supporting a building.

Rupee The unit of currency in India and many parts of Southeast Asia. The name means 'silver coin'.

Translucent Letting light shine through.

Urdu The official language of the Mughal Empire.

Whey A thin, clear, sour liquid produced when milk is curdled (turned sour) with acid. Curds (lumps or flakes) are produced at the same time, and can be pressed together to make cheese.

Index